I AM Because HE is the Great I AM

I AM Because HE is the Great I AM

Spirit-filled & Inspirational Decrees to Awaken, Empower, and Motivate Girls & Women from All Walks of Life

CARLA BOSTON

I AM Because He is the Great I AM—Spirit-filled & Inspirational Decrees to Awaken, Empower, and Motivate Girls & Women from All Walks of Life by Carla Boston

Cover design, editing, book layout, and publishing services by KishKnows, Inc., Richton Park, Illinois, 708-252-DOIT admin@kishknows.com, www.kishknows.com

ISBN 978-0-578-55682-6

LCCN 2019911267

All rights reserved. No part of this book may be reproduced, distributed, or transmitted in any form or by any means, including photocopying, recording, digital scanning, or other electronic or mechanical methods, without the prior written permission of the publisher, except in the case of brief quotations embodied in critical reviews and certain other noncommercial uses permitted by copyright law. For permission requests, please contact Carla Boston at peacecoolcarla@yahoo.com.

Some Scripture references may be paraphrased versions or illustrative references of the author. Unless otherwise indicated, all Scripture quotations are taken from the Holy Bible, New Living Translation (NLT), copyright © 1996, 2004, 2015 by Tyndale House Foundation. Used by permission of Tyndale House Publishers, Inc., Carol Stream, Illinois 60188. All rights reserved.

Scriptures noted as KJV are taken from the King James Version®. The King James Version is in the public domain in the United States.

Copyright © 2019 by Carla Boston

Chicago, Illinois

Printed in the United States of America.

CONTENTS

From a Friend… vii
Preface..xi
I AM Decrees… 1
Thanks…Acknowledgments… Inspirations… ...79
About the Author 81
Contact the Author 83

From a Friend...

"If you're to enter into God's Kingdom, you must believe that I am what I am. I am the Light of the World. I am the Prince of Peace. I am the Bread of Life and I am the Eternal Light. I am the door at which you must enter, you must believe that I am what I am."

These are verses from a song that I heard at a young age. It was the first song that I sang solo in church or anywhere, and I remember my grandmother, Fairy, coaching and encouraging me to sing this song. I finally did one Sunday, and I recall singing it so fast because I was nervous. It has held a place in my heart ever since.

I am a child of God. I am free, beautiful, and a mother of nations. Forgiven. An overcomer, an example, an heiress, a lender. Sinless, self-controlled, forgiven, pure, loving, faithful, peaceful, joyous…and *saved*. I am all of the things that my Father who resides in Heaven says. These are all characteristics of Him. I am in Him and He is in me.

During the time of my acknowledging who I am in Christ, so many things have happened. My husband got a new job. I have found peace spiritually, mentally, and physically. I have found a renewed strength in all aspects of life. My family is engaging more with each other. There has been an abundance of love, peace, encouragement, joy, teamwork, and praying. We have had an increase in health, positive mindsets, and building our relationship with the Lord more as a family.

Reading this manual will be inspirational, empowering, and equipping to anyone who reads it. We have all experienced life: love, divorce, marriage, illness, parenting, death, financial ups and downs, rebirth, battles of faith, relocations, employment, and health issues. However, we are all mighty according to the Word of God. We are powerful and mighty!

This reading is for you! God bless you! We are all in this together as long as the Lord is first! I love you, sister.

~ Tunisha Williams
Rantoul, Illinois

I AM Because He is the Great I AM

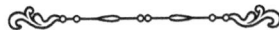

I AM my sister's friend and keeper.

Psalm 27:17: Iron Sharpens Iron,
One person sharpens another,
and I am my sister's keeper.

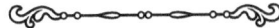

Preface

The purpose of this manual is to…

- inspire and awaken that which may be slumbering within the mind, body, and soul of a woman.

- enlighten the minds of women all over the world as it relates to being a daughter.

- encourage women to embrace their true identity and experience the heart and love of a Father and Creator according to the Living Word of God.

Psalm 139:14 (NLT): "Thank you for making me so wonderfully complex! Your workmanship is marvelous—how well I know it."

Every woman (including me!) should be excited to tap into the godly confidence that the writer had when this verse was written. The writer knew that they were "wonderfully made," and that the workmanship of the Creator is marvelous beyond a shadow of a doubt.

I believe by faith that through the reading of this manual, many readers will begin to allow the thoughts of their Creator to define them and allow the Living Word to become their reality.

Filled with empowering decrees, this little handbook is for mental and spiritual growth and development as it relates to your personal identity and relationship with the Creator of Heaven and Earth. As you begin to read, study, and apply the contents of the manual, you will find yourself unlocking deeper truths about yourself and your Creator. An openness to learn and a willingness to change your thinking will be a great asset to receiving the information contained in this "quick-read manual."

This manual is also an activation, and there is a measure of responsibility on your part to implement and build up a discipline in many areas of your life in order to see fruitful results.

Be open and your thinking will be challenged!

I AM Because He is the Great I AM

Instructions:

- *Read this manual at your own pace.*
- Be open minded.
- *As you read each decree, study the Living Word reference for that day.*
- On those hard and challenging days, speak the words contained in this manual out loud, and apply what you speak to your life.
- *During your reading and study time, incorporate prayer and journaling. Set some time out of your day for meditation.*
- Set some personal goals and search for opportunities to apply what you gain from using this manual.
- *Watch how your mind and life begin to change for the better.*

I AM Decrees…

DECREE 1

Ephesians 3:18: "And may you have the power to understand, as all God's people should, how high, and how deep his love is."

I AM my Father's daughter. His love for me goes beyond what my mind could ever comprehend in this life, and nothing in this world can separate me from that love. (You should be shouting for JOY!) The writer is convinced…and so shall you be, if you continue to read and believe!

DECREE 2

Psalm 139:14: "Thank you for making me so wonderfully complex! Your workmanship is marvelous—how well I know it."

I AM fearfully and wonderfully made in the image of my Father.

___
___
___
___
___
___
___
___

Decree 3

> *2 Peter 1:4: "And because of his glory and excellence, he has given us great and precious promises. These are the promises that enable you to share his divine nature and escape the world's corruption caused by human desires."*

I AM a partaker in the divine nature of my Father.

DECREE 4

Ephesians 3:17: "Then Christ will make his home in your hearts as you trust in him. Your roots will grow down into God's love and keep you strong."

I AM rooted and grounded in love.

_____
_____
_____
_____
_____
_____
_____
_____

Decree 5

Luke 2:52: "Jesus grew in wisdom and in stature and in favor with God and all the people."

I AM a woman who is growing in wisdom and stature and in favor with God and man. (Consider the simple addition and multiplication in this text, and think about how to apply it to your life)

_____
_____
_____
_____
_____
_____
_____
_____

DECREE 6

1 Peter 2:9: *"But you are not like that, for you are a chosen people. You are royal priests, a holy nation, God's very own possession. As a result, you can show others the goodness of God, for he called you out of the darkness into his wonderful light."*

I AM a woman with a high degree of spiritual insight and character, a chosen nation, set apart, and not corrupted by influence or success.

_____
_____
_____
_____
_____
_____
_____
_____

DECREE 7

***John 15:16:** "You didn't choose me. I chose you. I appointed you to go and produce lasting fruit, so that the Father will give you whatever you ask for, using my name."*

I AM a woman of spiritual inspiration and activation because of what God has chosen me to do.

_____
_____
_____
_____
_____
_____
_____
_____

Decree 8

Proverbs 20:12: "Ears to hear and eyes to see—both are gifts from the Lord."

I AM equipped to bring cohesiveness into any situation.

_____
_____
_____
_____
_____
_____
_____
_____
_____

DECREE 9

***Psalm 111:10:** "Fear of the Lord is the foundation of true wisdom. All who obey his commandments will grow in wisdom."*

I AM a wise woman who has a connection *with* God and *to* God…and everybody knows it.

_____
_____
_____
_____
_____
_____
_____
_____
_____

DECREE 10

Revelation 19:10: "Then I fell down at his feet to worship him, but he said, 'No, don't worship me... Worship only God. For the essence of prophecy is to give a clear witness for Jesus.'"

I AM prophetic and able to discern the mind and purposes of God.

DECREE 11

***Acts 1:8:** "You will receive power when the Holy Spirit comes upon you. And you will be my witnesses, telling people about me everywhere—in Jerusalem, throughout Judea, in Samaria, and to the ends of the earth."*

I AM a servant of God, just like my fellow brothers and sisters who testify about their faith in Jesus.

_____
_____
_____
_____
_____
_____
_____
_____
_____

DECREE 12

Psalm 45:1: "Beautiful words stir my heart. I will recite a lovely poem about the king, for my tongue is like the pen of a skillful poet."

I AM a skilled woman with a learned tongue. I have a word to sustain myself and the weary-hearted.

_____
_____
_____
_____
_____
_____
_____
_____
_____
_____

DECREE 13

Proverbs 4:7: "Getting wisdom is the wisest thing you can do! And whatever else you do, develop good judgment."

I AM a woman of prophetic insight and wisdom.

_____
_____
_____
_____
_____
_____
_____
_____
_____

DECREE 14

***Hebrews 11:6: "It is impossible
to please God without faith."***

I AM a woman of godly authority and dominion, and I execute it properly by faith and obedience.

_____
_____
_____
_____
_____
_____
_____
_____
_____

DECREE 15

Isaiah 1:19: "If you will only obey me, you will have plenty to eat."

I AM a woman who submits and aligns herself to the prophetic order and protocols set and established by Yahweh.

_____
_____
_____
_____
_____
_____
_____
_____
_____

DECREE 16

Hebrews 13:1-2: "Keep on loving each other as brothers and sisters. Don't forget to show hospitality to strangers, for some who have done this have entertained angels without realizing it!"

I AM a lover of people.

_____
_____
_____
_____
_____
_____
_____
_____
_____

DECREE 17

Matthew 25:37-40: "Then these righteous ones will reply, 'Lord, when did we ever see you hungry and feed you? Or thirsty and give you something to drink? Or a stranger and show you hospitality? Or naked and give you clothing? When did we ever see you sick or in prison and visit you?' And the King will say, 'I tell you the truth, when you did it to one of the least of these my brothers and sisters, you were doing it to me!'"

I AM a woman who is continually learning how to minister and serve the Lord through serving His people.

_____
_____
_____
_____
_____
_____
_____
_____
_____

DECREE 18

Isaiah 53:5: "But he was pierced for our rebellion, crushed for our sins. He was beaten so we could be whole. He was whipped so we could be healed."

I AM a woman who is healed by the stripes of Christ. (Why would anyone struggle with believing in an infinite power who has done all of that for *us*?)

DECREE 19

Psalm 133:1: "How wonderful and pleasant it is when brothers live together in harmony!"

I AM a woman who continually seeks to dwell in harmony, both with myself and with others.

_____
_____
_____
_____
_____
_____
_____
_____
_____

DECREE 20

Proverbs 11:1: "The Lord detests the use of dishonest scales, but he delights in accurate weights."

I AM a woman who seeks balance and stability in every area of my life, including but not limited to the following…

Mental • Physical • Emotional • Spiritual
• Natural • Relational • Financial

_____
_____
_____
_____
_____
_____
_____
_____
_____

DECREE 21

Psalm 141:3: "Take control of what I say, O Lord, and guard my lips."

I AM a woman with a listening ear, a quiet and guarded mouth, and an understanding mind and heart.

___
___
___
___
___
___
___
___

DECREE 22

James 1:4 (KJV): "Let patience have her perfect work, that ye may be perfect and entire, wanting nothing."

I AM a woman of great grace, patience, and virtue.

_____
_____
_____
_____
_____
_____
_____
_____
_____

Decree 23

Proverbs 31:25 (KJV): "She is clothed with strength and dignity, and she laughs without fear of the future."

I AM a well-postured woman.

DECREE 24

Proverbs 31:16-18: "She goes to inspect a field and buys it; with her earnings she plants a vineyard. She is energetic and strong, a hard worker. She makes sure her dealings are profitable; her lamp burns late into the night."

I AM a beautiful and intellectual woman with a keen sense of business.

___
___
___
___
___
___
___
___
___

DECREE 25

Nehemiah 8:10: "The joy of the Lord is your strength."

I AM a free and joyful woman.

_____
_____
_____
_____
_____
_____
_____
_____
_____

DECREE 26

***John 4:24: "For God is Spirit,
so those who worship him must
worship in spirit and in truth."***

I AM a woman of Holy Spirit-filled worship and inspired praise.

DECREE 27

Romans 8:27: "And the Father who knows all hearts knows what the Spirit is saying, for the Spirit pleads for us believers in harmony with God's own will."

I AM not a woman who is driven by my emotions…I am a woman led by the Holy Spirit.

_____
_____
_____
_____
_____
_____
_____
_____
_____

Decree 28

Colossians 3:12: "Since God chose you to be the holy people he loves, you must clothe yourselves with tenderhearted mercy, kindness, humility, gentleness, and patience."

I AM a woman of humility and modesty.

DECREE 29

Matthew 5:9: "God blesses those who work for peace, for they will be called the children of God."

I AM a peacemaker.

DECREE 30

James 2:17: *"So you see, faith by itself isn't enough. Unless it produces good deeds, it is dead and useless."*

I AM an intercessor and I act upon my prayers to the Father because I understand that faith without action is dead.

DECREE 31

***Romans 8:38:** "And I am convinced that nothing can ever separate us from God's love. Neither death nor life, neither angels or demons, neither our fears about today nor our worries about tomorrow—not even the powers of hell can separate us from God's love."*

I am Valuable and nothing can separate me from my Father's Love.

DECREE 32

***Romans 12:10:** "Love each other with genuine affection and take delight in honoring each other."*

I AM a gift to many and I love to see people happy…including myself.

_____
_____
_____
_____
_____
_____
_____
_____
_____

DECREE 33

Proverbs 31:20: "She extends a helping hand to the poor and opens her arms to the needy."

I AM a woman who cares about the welfare of others.

_____
_____
_____
_____
_____
_____
_____
_____
_____

DECREE 34

***Isaiah 10:27:** "In that day the Lord will end the bondage of his people. He will break the yoke of slavery and lift it from their shoulders."*

I AM anointed with the power to destroy and remove strongholds and strongmen set in place to keep me bound.

___
___
___
___
___
___
___
___
___

Decree 35

***Esther 4:14:** "Who knows if perhaps you were made queen for just such a time as this?"*

I AM often at the right place, at the right time, using the right weapons for warfare.

DECREE 36

Acts 17:28 (KJV): "For in him we live, and move, and have our being."

I AM a woman who lives beyond man-made expectations and rejects limitations.

_____
_____
_____
_____
_____
_____
_____
_____
_____

DECREE 37

Ephesians 4:7 (KJV): "But unto every one of us is given grace according to the measure of the gift of Christ."

I AM a woman of boldness and accuracy according to the measure of grace given to me by Yahweh.

DECREE 38

> *Isaiah 61:1: "The Spirit of the Sovereign Lord is upon me, for the Lord has anointed me to bring good news to the poor. He has sent me to comfort the brokenhearted and to proclaim that captives will be released, and prisoners will be freed."*

I AM a woman who possesses keys to release myself and others from bondage and into a place of freedom and liberty.

DECREE 39

Luke 4:18-19: "The spirit of the LORD is upon me... to bring Good News to the poor. He has sent me to proclaim that captives will be released, that the blind will see, that the oppressed will be set free, and that the time of the LORD's favor has come."

I AM free from the oppressor and oppression.

DECREE 40

Acts 2:43: "A deep sense of awe came over them all, and the apostles performed many miraculous signs and wonders."

I AM a vessel of supernatural signs, miracles, and wonders, manifested and demonstrated.

_____
_____
_____
_____
_____
_____
_____
_____
_____

Decree 41

> *1 Peter 4:10: "God has given each of you a gift from his great variety of spiritual gifts. Use them well to serve one another."*

I AM a woman whose skills, gifts, and talents are being used for the glory of the Kingdom of God.

DECREE 42

Psalm 127:3: "Children are a gift from the Lord; they are a reward from him."

I AM family oriented.

_____
_____
_____
_____
_____
_____
_____
_____
_____

DECREE 43

Isaiah 52:2: *"Rise from the dust, O Jerusalem. Sit in a place of honor. Remove the chains of slavery from your neck, O captive daughter of Zion."*

I AM a daughter of Zion.

_____
_____
_____
_____
_____
_____
_____
_____
_____

DECREE 44

Isaiah 43:18-19: "But forget all that—it is nothing compared to what I am going to do. For I am about to do something new. See, I have already begun! Do you not see it? I will make a pathway through the wilderness. I will create rivers in the dry wasteland."

I AM a woman of healing and deliverance.

DECREE 45

Proverbs 31:10: "Who can find a virtuous and capable wife?"

I AM a wife of noble character.

DECREE 46

1 John 3:8: "But when people keep on sinning, it shows that they belong to the devil, who has been sinning since the beginning. But the Son of God came to destroy the works of the devil."

I AM a woman who has purposed herself to destroy the works of the devil because Christ lives in me.

_____
_____
_____
_____
_____
_____
_____
_____
_____

DECREE 47

> *1 Thessalonians 5:23: "Now may the God of peace make you holy in every way, and may your whole spirit and soul and body be kept blameless until our Lord Jesus Christ comes again."*

I AM a whole and holy woman.

DECREE 48

***Jeremiah 17:14:** "O Lord, if you heal me, I will be truly healed; if you save me, I will be truly saved. My praises are for you alone!"*

I AM no longer emotionally broken…I have been made whole.

_____
_____
_____
_____
_____
_____
_____
_____

DECREE 49

***Romans 5:8:** "But God showed his great love for us by sending Christ to die for us while we were still sinners."*

I AM a woman who is accepted by God the Father.

_____
_____
_____
_____
_____
_____
_____
_____
_____

DECREE 50

Micah 6:8: "No, O people, the Lord has told you what is good, and this is what he requires of you: to do what is right, to love mercy, and to walk humbly with your God."

I AM a woman who shows mercy and upholds justice.

_____
_____
_____
_____
_____
_____
_____
_____
_____

DECREE 51

Isaiah 60:17: "I will exchange your bronze for gold, your iron for silver, your wood for bronze, and your stones for iron. I will make peace your leader and righteousness your ruler."

I AM a woman who is governed by peace and ruled by righteousness.

DECREE 52

Psalm 119:30: "I have chosen to be faithful; I have determined to live by your regulations."

I AM a woman of godly fortitude and faith.

DECREE 53

> *Mark 12:30: "And you must love the Lord your God with all your heart, all your soul, all your mind, and all your strength."*

I AM a woman who walks and thinks in love, in power, and with a sound mind.

DECREE 54

***James 1:6:** "But when you ask him, be sure that your faith is in God alone. Do not waver, for a person with divided loyalty is as unsettled as a wave of the sea that is blown and tossed by the wind."*

I AM not tossed to and fro with every wind of doctrine or opinions.

Decree 55

> *Mark 8:34: "Then, calling the crowd to join his disciples, he said, 'If any of you wants to be my follower, you must give up your own way, take up your cross, and follow me.'"*

I AM not enslaved to my environmental beliefs (social circles, professional circles, or family).

_____
_____
_____
_____
_____
_____
_____
_____
_____

DECREE 56

***John 1:17:** "For the law was given through Moses, but God's unfailing love and faithfulness came through Jesus Christ."*

I AM a woman who is released from restrictions imposed by people.

_____
_____
_____
_____
_____
_____
_____
_____

DECREE 57

Philippians 4:8: "And now, dear brothers and sisters, one final thing. Fix your thoughts on what is true, and honorable, and right, and pure, and lovely, and admirable. Think about things that are excellent and worthy of praise."

I AM free from ungodly mindsets and beliefs.

DECREE 58

Psalm 118:6: "The Lord is for me, so I will have no fear. What can mere people do to me?"

I AM a woman who embraces Truth. I DO NOT accept lies or agree with anything contrary to the truth of God's Word concerning me.

DECREE 59

Proverbs 24:26: "An honest answer is like a kiss of friendship."

I AM a woman who speaks the truth in love.

DECREE 60

Romans 12:2: "Don't copy the behavior and customs of this world, but let God transform you into a new person by changing the way you think. Then you will learn to know God's will for you, which is good and pleasing and perfect."

I AM a woman with a renewed mind.

DECREE 61

2 Peter 1:19-21: "Because of that experience, we have even greater confidence in the message proclaimed by the prophets. You must pay close attention to what they wrote, for their words are like a lamp shining in a dark place—until the Day dawns, and Christ the Morning Star shines in your hearts. Above all, you must realize that no prophecy in Scripture ever came from the prophet's own understanding, or from human initiative. No, those prophets were moved by the Holy Spirit, and they spoke from God."

I AM a woman of great revelation, both spiritually and naturally.

___
___
___
___
___
___
___
___
___

DECREE 62

***Romans 12:6:** "In his grace, God has given us different gifts for doing certain things well."*

I AM creative, innovative, and full of witty inventions.

DECREE 63

Colossians 3:23-24: "Work willingly at whatever you do, as though you were working for the Lord rather than for people. Remember that the Lord will give you an inheritance as your reward, and that the Master you are serving is Christ."

I AM wholesome, truthful, and productive.

___
___
___
___
___
___
___
___

DECREE 64

***Isaiah 26:3: "You will keep in perfect
peace all who trust in you,
all whose thoughts are fixed on you!"***

I AM steadfast and unmovable.

_____
_____
_____
_____
_____
_____
_____
_____
_____

DECREE 65

1 Thessalonians 5:11: *"So, encourage each other and build each other up, just as you are already doing."*

I AM a nurturer.

_____
_____
_____
_____
_____
_____
_____
_____
_____

DECREE 66

> **2 Corinthians 5:17:** *"This means that anyone who belongs to Christ has become a new person. The old life is gone; a new life has begun!"*

I AM *not* defined by my past mistakes.

DECREE 67

Philippians 3:20: "But we are citizens of heaven, where the Lord Jesus Christ lives. And we are eagerly waiting for him to return as our Savior."

I AM who the Word of God says I am.

DECREE 68

***Ephesians 6:10:** "A final word: Be strong in the Lord and in his mighty power."*

I AM strong in the Lord and in the power of His might.

DECREE 69

Colossians 3:8: "But now is the time to get rid of anger, rage, malicious behavior, slander, and dirty language."

I AM not a gossiper, murmurer, or complainer.

Decree 70

2 Timothy 2:15: (KJV): "Study to show thyself approved unto God, a workman that needeth not to be ashamed, rightly dividing the word of truth."

I AM well-studied and well-versed in the things of my Heavenly Father.

DECREE 71

> *Galatians 5:22-23: "But the Holy Spirit produces this kind of fruit in our lives: love, joy, peace, patience, kindness, goodness and faithfulness, gentleness, and self-control."*

I AM a woman who bears the fruit of humility and self-control.

DECREE 72

***Psalm 144:1:** "Praise the Lord, who is my rock. He trains my hands for war and gives my fingers skill for battle."*

I AM a well-equipped woman of war and victory, and I choose my battles wisely.

_____
_____
_____
_____
_____
_____
_____
_____
_____

DECREE 73

John 14:14: "Yes, ask me for anything in my name, and I will do it!"

I AM a woman who prays in line with the Holy Spirit.

———————————————————
———————————————————
———————————————————
———————————————————
———————————————————
———————————————————
———————————————————
———————————————————
———————————————————

DECREE 74

***Genesis 1:26:** "Then God said, 'Let us make human beings[a] in our image, to be like us. They will reign over the fish in the sea, the birds in the sky, the livestock, all the wild animals on the earth,[b] and the small animals that scurry along the ground.'"*

I AM created in the Image of my Father.

Decree 75

Psalm 95:6-7: "Come, let us worship and bow down. Let us kneel before the Lord our maker, for he is our God. We are the people he watches over, the flock under his care."

I AM a woman who worships only God, for the essence of prophecy is to give a clear witness for Jesus.

THANKS...
ACKNOWLEDGMENTS...
INSPIRATIONS...

As I sit here and type, thinking of the different people, places, and things that inspired me to write this book, the song *"I'll Always Love My Mama, She's My Favorite Girl"* by The Intruders comes to mind. If you are not familiar with this song, you should look it up…the words are very powerful!

My mother, Anita Hagan, is my greatest motivation and inspiration outside of my Heavenly Father. I remember when she would do my hair as a little cub, she would whisper in my ear, "Baby, you can do anything you want to do and go anywhere you want to go." Those words spoken so eloquently and softly in my ear became the cornerstone of my dreams and aspirations. She also introduced me to Christ through frequent fellowship and church community involvement.

Being introduced to Christ in that manner laid a foundation for a way of life. I am eternally grateful to my Heavenly Father for blessing me with such a woman.

I also thank my aunts and uncles who often shared words of correction and wisdom with me and my cousins at such a young age and continue to do so even now. Those seeds continue to grow and produce fruit in my life. God knew exactly what He was doing when He chose my family!

My four young kings: I am delighted and amazed at how God uses them to keep me in line. Their love, respect, and appreciation for me makes my life worth living. I am forever thankful for having such blessed and strong young men to raise and love.

My sisters and brothers in Christ who continue to love me and hold me accountable, along with my dear friends who are always there to listen and support, even when they didn't feel up to it. I am thankful to them, for they help to keep me grounded.

My Heavenly Father, my friend and lover of my soul. He *is* and *will always* be the reason I praise, give thanks and reverence for allowing me to be ME, in all of my essence.

My darling Darryl…my friend, brother, protector, provider, and king. Having you in my life has ignited a child-like faith and hope in me that I have never experienced before. I am thankful to my Father for allowing you and me to reconnect. You sharpen me and keep me on my toes, and God knew how much I needed that from my partner.

ABOUT THE AUTHOR

I was born in Chicago, Illinois, on the south side of town. Being raised in a house full of guys afforded me a lot of strength. I am a firm believer that the strength of a woman comes from a man. I was eighteen months old when I lost my mother. She was only twenty-one when she passed away. Losing my mom at such a young age put me in a situation that I had no control over. Thankfully, my mothers' siblings took me in and raised me. I was the only girl in a house full of boys. I was obviously too young to know what was happening, but I can remember being sad a lot as a little girl. The bond between a mother and child is strong.

My mother's eldest sister Anita and her husband George took me in and cared for me like their own. I was sent to a Catholic school from kindergarten through eighth grade, and they introduced me to Christ at a very young age, which became the cornerstone for my life. Knowing the Lord and His Word helped me through a lot of life's challenges and trials. When trouble came, my anchor was and will always be my Heavenly Father.

Throughout my teenage years and young adulthood, despite social, economic, and emotional challenges, I've always managed to overcome. Today, I can confidently say that it was all because of my relationship with my Father God. He has sustained me through it all and He still continues to do so. The only thing I can take ownership of is my Faith in Him—He did the rest.

I am a divorcee. I was married for 18 years, and I have four strong young men. Recently, by the grace and love of God, I am happily married again after being divorced for six years. I serve as a youth leader at my church and I am the store manager of a hair-cutting franchise. In the past, I've owned and operated two hair salons. Along with being a licensed cosmetologist, I am also a licensed and registered Medical Assistant and a phlebotomist through Kaplan College.

Currently, I am an aspiring writer and a full-time college student pursuing a degree in business.

CONTACT THE AUTHOR

Email: peacecoolcarla@yahoo.com
Facebook: Carla Cool C

www.ingramcontent.com/pod-product-compliance
Lightning Source LLC
Chambersburg PA
CBHW071410290426
44108CB00014B/1762